D0575531

Backyard Animals

Lynx

Blaine Wiseman

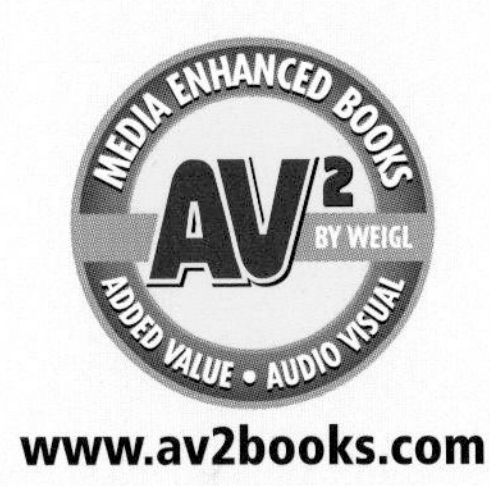

www.av2books.com

BOOK CODE

K775763

AV² by Weigl brings you media enhanced books that support active learning.

AV² provides enriched content that supplements and complements this book. Weigl's AV² books strive to create inspired learning and engage young minds for a total learning experience.

Go to **www.av2books.com**, and enter this book's unique code. You will have access to video, audio, web links, quizzes, a slide show, and activities.

Audio
Listen to sections of the book read aloud.

Video
Watch informative video clips.

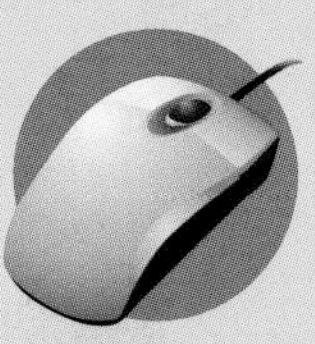

Web Link
Find research sites and play interactive games.

Try This!
Complete activities and hands-on experiments.

Due to the dynamic nature of the Internet, some of the URLs and activities provided as part of AV² by Weigl may have changed or ceased to exist. AV² by Weigl accepts no responsibility for any such changes. All media enhanced books are regularly monitored to update addresses and sites in a timely manner. Contact AV² by Weigl at 1-866-649-3445 or av2books@weigl.com with any questions, comments, or feedback.

Published by AV² by Weigl
350 5th Avenue, 59th Floor
New York, NY 10118
Website: www.av2books.com   www.weigl.com

Library of Congress Cataloging-in-Publication Data

Wiseman, Blaine.
Lynx / Blaine Wiseman.
p. cm. -- (Backyard animals)
Includes index.
ISBN 978-1-60596-943-5 (hardcover : alk. paper) -- ISBN 978-1-60596-944-2 (softcover : alk. paper) --
ISBN 978-1-60596-945-9 (e-book)
1. Lynx (Genus)--Juvenile literature. I. Title.
QL737.C23W57 2010
599.75'3--dc22
2009050955

Printed in the United States of America in North Mankato, Minnesota
2 3 4 5 6 7 8 9 15 14 13 12 11

102011
WEP211011

Editor Heather C. Hudak   **Design** Terry Paulhus

Every reasonable effort has been made to trace ownership and to obtain permission to reprint copyright material. The publishers would be pleased to have any errors or omissions brought to their attention so that they may be corrected in subsequent printings.

Photo Credits
Weigl acknowledges Getty Images as its primary photo supplier for this title.

Contents

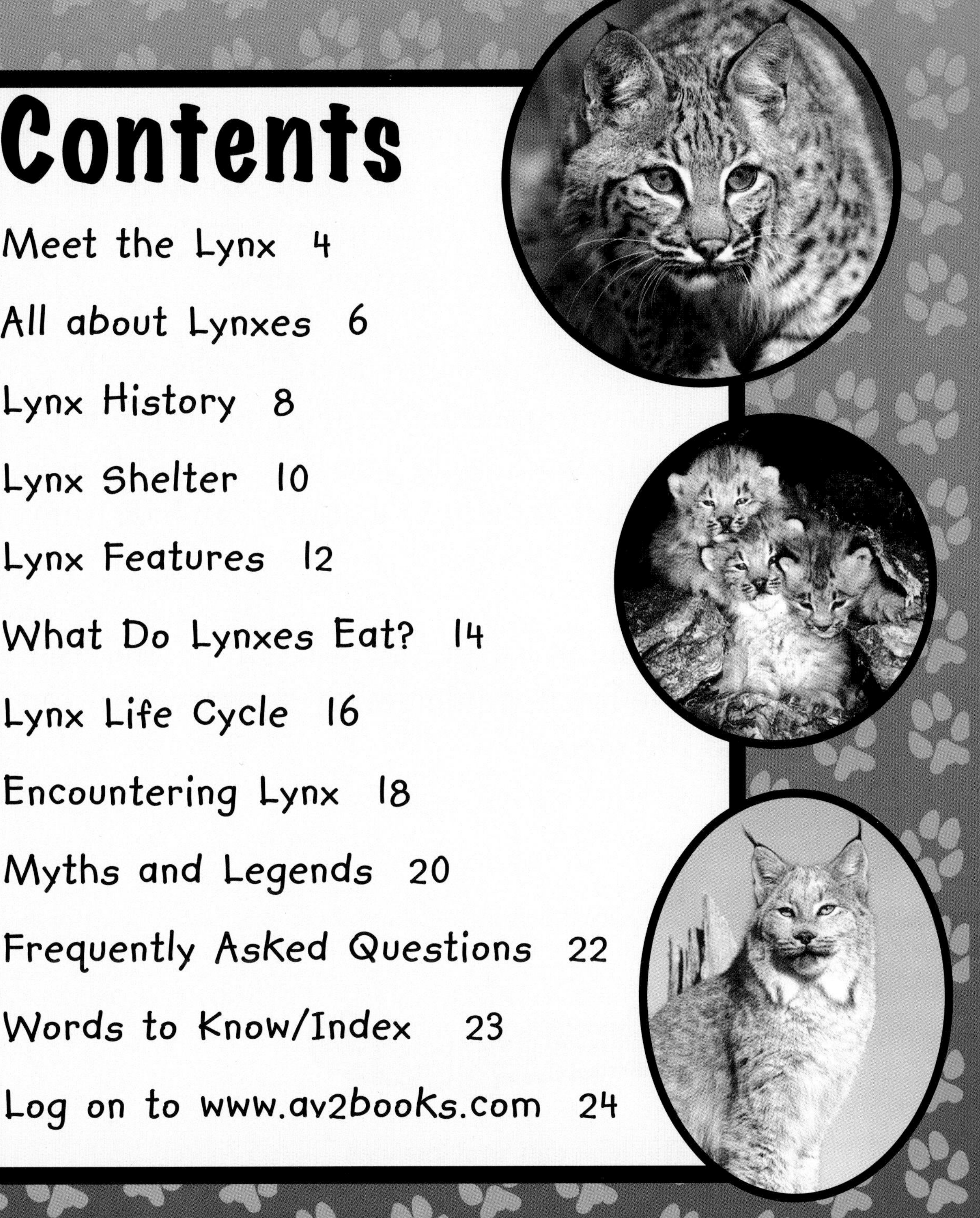

Meet the Lynx

Lynxes are **mammals**. They are wild cats that have long legs, large paws, and long tufts of hair on top of their ears. Lynxes have excellent hearing and eyesight, and can move very quickly across thick snow.

Very thick fur covers the lynx's body. This fur helps keep these cats warm during winter. The fur is often a dull color with black spots. This help lynxes blend in to their **habitat** at night so that they can hide from their **prey**.

Lynxes are found in North America, Europe, and Asia. They prefer to live in mountain forests where they can find food and shelter.

The lynx can spot prey as small as a mouse from 250 feet (76.2 meters) away.

The color of a lynx's fur helps it blend in with its surroundings.

All about Lynxes

There are four **species** of lynx. These are the Canada lynx, the Eurasian lynx, the Iberian lynx, and the bobcat. All four species have thick fur, long hind legs, short tails, and furry faces and ears. However, each species has special features as well. For example, they grow to different sizes.

A Siberian lynx is a type of Eurasian lynx found in Russia. It can weigh up to 84 pounds (38 kilograms). Meanwhile, most full-grown bobcats weigh about 15 to 28 pounds (7 to 13 kg). Females can weigh as little as 9 pounds (4 kg).

Lynx mothers often purr while grooming their kittens. This is a sign that they are feeling calm.

Sizes of Lynx

Canada Lynx	Eurasian Lynx
• Weighs between 10 and 38 pounds (4.5 and 17.3 kg) • Males are slightly larger than females.	• Weighs between 40 and 84 pounds (18.1 and 38 kg) • The largest lynx species, and the largest type of cat in Europe
Iberian Lynx	**Bobcat**
• Weighs between 21 and 59 pounds (9.3 and 26.8 kg)	• Weighs between 9 and 33 pounds (4 and 15 kg) • Smallest member of the lynx family

Lynx History

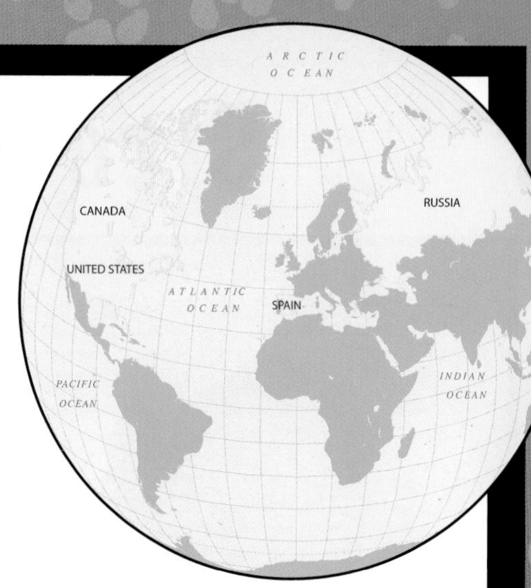

The earliest known lynx, the Issoire lynx, lived around 4 million years ago. It looked like a big house cat and was bigger than any species of lynx today.

In the past, lynxes were more common than they are today. However, their numbers dropped when people began hunting lynxes for their fur. Today, some types of lynx are protected in the United States. However, humans are still the main threat to lynxes. Building roads and communities destroys lynx habitats and makes life more difficult for these cats.

The Iberian lynx, which lives in Spain, is the world's most **endangered** cat. There are fewer than 150 Iberian lynxes left. Humans have overhunted their main prey, the rabbit. This has left very little food for the Iberian lynx.

Fascinating Facts

Scientists in Spain found a group of Iberian lynx that had never been seen before. They hope that there are other lynx hiding in the country.

Some people hunt lynxes for their beautiful fur. This threatens their survival.

Lynx Shelter

Lynxes live in thick forests with many trees and shrubs so that they can hide from other animals. This allows them to sneak up on their prey. Lynxes live under rocks or fallen trees, or inside caves or hollow logs. A lynx chooses its **den** carefully. A den must be warm and shelter the cat from poor weather, humans, and animals. It must also be close to the lynx's hunting area.

Except for a mother lynx and her kittens, lynxes prefer to live alone. Each lynx has its own territory, where other lynx do not roam. A territory can range from 4 to 100 square miles (10.4 to 259 square kilometers).

Lynx kittens live the first few months of their lives in a den their mother finds.

Adult lynxes rarely seek shelter. They may use trees, caves, or rock ledges to protect them from harsh weather.

Lynx Features

All lynx share the same basic features. For example, a lynx's hind legs are longer than its front legs. Bobcats can use their long legs to jump more than 10 feet (3 meters) through the air. This is useful for pouncing on prey.

TAIL
Most cats have a long tail that helps them balance. A snow leopard's tail can be as long as 3 feet (1 meter). Lynxes have very short tails. Some are only 4 inches (10 centimeters) long. Bobcats are named for their short, or "bobbed," tail.

EARS
Lynxes have long tufts of black hair on top of their ears. These hairs help the lynx hear very quiet sounds.

EYES
Lynxes have excellent eyesight. This helps them hunt in forests at night. Lynxes rely mostly on their eyesight to find prey.

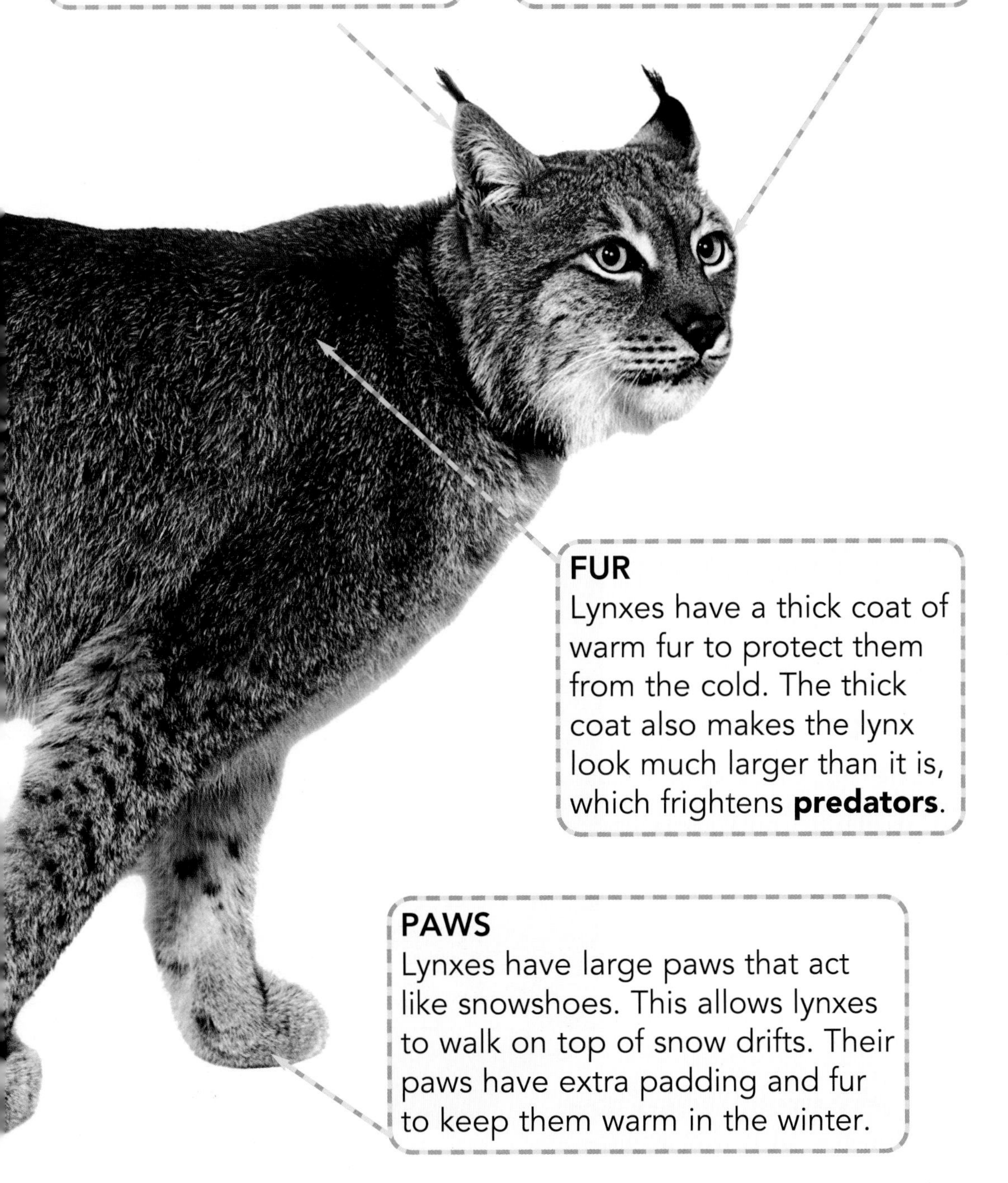

FUR
Lynxes have a thick coat of warm fur to protect them from the cold. The thick coat also makes the lynx look much larger than it is, which frightens **predators**.

PAWS
Lynxes have large paws that act like snowshoes. This allows lynxes to walk on top of snow drifts. Their paws have extra padding and fur to keep them warm in the winter.

What Do Lynxes Eat?

Lynxes are **carnivores**. They mainly eat small animals, such as birds and rodents. A favorite food of the Canada lynx is the snowshoe hare. Siberian lynx, however, hunt prey as large as deer.

All lynxes hunt. They slowly creep up on their prey. Padded feet help lynxes move very quietly. Sometimes, a lynx will wait hours before pouncing on its food. The lynx's special jumping ability helps it catch prey quickly without a chase.

Some lynxes hunt in a group. One lynx frightens the prey away, while another lynx traps the animal. Female lynxes use this method to teach their young how to hunt.

Some very strong lynxes have been known to prey on animals as large as reindeer.

Lynxes have wide paws that make it easy for them to move over snow.

Lynx Life Cycle

The only time that a male lynx will meet with another lynx is during the late winter or early spring. This is mating season for lynxes.

Birth

Lynx kittens are born with fuzzy, streaked fur. Their eyes are closed and ears folded. The kittens are unable to see or hear. Lynx kittens weigh less than 1 pound (0.45 kg) and can fit in the palm of a human hand.

1 day to 5 months

For the first five months, lynx kittens stay inside or close to their den. They feed only on their mother's milk. The mother takes care of all the kittens' needs and protects them from predators.

Male lynxes mate with the females that live nearby. The females give birth to kittens about two months later. Each female gives birth to a **litter** of one to eight kittens per year. An average litter is two to four kittens.

6 months to 1 year

After six months, lynx kittens begin learning how to hunt. The kittens stay with their mother for about one year before leaving to take care of themselves.

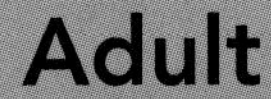

Adult

Lynxes reach their adult size at about two years of age. Once they have left their mother's den, lynxes must hunt for themselves and find their own den. Two siblings will sometimes stay together for a short time before going their separate ways.

Encountering Lynx

People rarely encounter lynxes in their daily lives. Lynxes are most active at night and prefer to stay away from humans. However, people sometimes see lynxes while camping or hiking in forests and mountains.

Lynxes are not tame and can be dangerous. For this reason, it is important not to approach a lynx. If a person sees an injured or ill lynx, a wildlife officer should be called for help. Injured animals are often scared, making them more likely to attack.

Feeding a lynx can make the animal want to be near people. It may begin coming into campsites in search of food. This can be harmful to people who may encounter the animal, and is not healthy for the lynx.

Fascinating Facts

Lynxes can only run fast for a short distance. If a rabbit avoids a lynx's first pounce, it can often outrun the lynx and get away. Lynxes have to sneak up on their prey to catch it.

Like most cats, lynxes have a very good sense of balance.

Myths and Legends

Since lynxes are rarely found near humans, there are few myths and legends. Thousands of years ago, the ancient Greeks began telling myths about the lynx. In one of these myths, Lynceus, or Lynx, was said to have the best eyesight in the world. His eyesight was so good that he could see in the darkness of the **underworld**.

Johannes Hevelius was an **astronomer** who studied the stars without using a telescope. Other astronomers said that he had the eyes of a lynx because he could see the stars so well. In 1687, Hevelius discovered a **constellation** that was made up of dimly lit stars. He called it "the lynx" because a person would need the sight of a lynx to see it without a telescope.

The word lynx comes from the Greek word, "to shine." This may be because of the way a lynx's eyes shine at night.

Achaanwaapush

This is a Cree legend about a rabbit that ate other animals. His name was Achaanwaapush.

One day, a family of lynxes camped near where Achaanwaapush lived. Before the mother and father lynx went out to hunt, they warned their children that Achaanwaapush would visit. They told their children he would ask them to scratch and soothe him. They said the children should use their claws to hurt him.

Achaanwaapush found the children and told them to scratch his back. He asked them to use their claws to scratch harder. They did as they were told.

As the lynx parents drew near the camp, they could tell that Achaanwaapush had been there. They feared he had eaten their children. The father was ready to fight, but he soon learned that the children had used their claws to kill the rabbit. They had saved the forest animals from his terrible ways.

Frequently Asked Questions

Do lynxes make sounds?

Answer: Lynxes make sounds similar to house cats. They use these sounds to communicate. Mother lynxes are known to purr while they take care of their kittens. Lynxes can also meow, yowl, growl, and hiss.

What is the difference between a lynx and a bobcat?

Answer: A bobcat is the smallest type of lynx. The bobcat has a longer tail, smaller feet, and shorter ear tufts than other types of lynx. One way to spot a bobcat is to look for black streaks along its tail rather than a solid black tip.

What do lynx tracks look like?

Answer: Lynxes make tracks in the snow similar to a mountain lion. However, their tracks are not as deep because their feet do not sink into the snow. As well, the tracks should show that the front feet are larger than the hind feet. Lynx tracks do not have claw marks because their claws are **retractable**.

Words to Know

astronomer: a person who studies the stars and planets
carnivores: meat-eating animals who hunt prey
constellation: a collection of stars that resembles an object or person in the sky
den: the home of an animal
endangered: at risk of becoming extinct
habitat: the parts of the world where an animal lives
litter: a group of kittens born together
mammals: warm-blooded, live-born animals that have a spine, fur or hair, and make milk for their young
predators: animals that hunt other animals for food
prey: an animal that is hunted by another animal
retractable: folded away when not being used
species: a group of similar animals that can breed together
underworld: in myths, an underground world where the dead live

Index

MEDIA ENHANCED BOOKS AV² BY WEIGL ADDED VALUE • AUDIO VISUAL

Log on to www.av2books.com

AV² by Weigl brings you media enhanced books that support active learning. Go to **www.av2books.com**, and enter the special code inside the front cover of this book. You will gain access to enriched and enhanced content that supplements and complements this book. Content includes video, audio, web links, quizzes, a slide show, and activities.

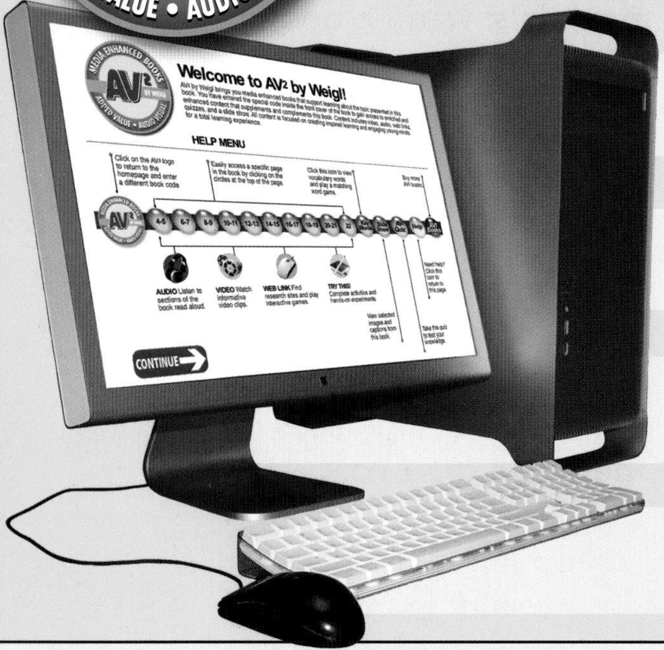

Audio
Listen to sections of the book read aloud.

Video
Watch informative video clips.

Web Link
Find research sites and play interactive games.

Try This!
Complete activities and hands-on experiments.

WHAT'S ONLINE?

Try This!
Complete activities and hands-on experiments.

Pages 6-7 Identify types of lynx.

Pages 12-13 List five important features of the lynx.

Pages 16-17 Compare the similarities and differences between a lynx kitten and an adult lynx.

Page 22 Test your lynx knowledge.

Web Link
Find research sites and play interactive games.

Pages 6-7 Find out more about lynx features.

Pages 8-9 Learn about the endangered Iberian lynx.

Pages 10-11 Play an interactive lynx game.

Pages 18-19 Find out fascinating facts about lynx.

Pages 20-21 Read more stories about lynx.

Video
Watch informative video clips.

Pages 4-5 Watch a video about Canada lynx.

Pages 10-11 See a lynx in its natural habitat.

Pages 14-15 Watch a video about lynx hunting prey.

EXTRA FEATURES

Audio
Hear introductory aud at the top of every pa

Key Words
Study vocabulary, and play a matching word game.

Slide Show
View images and captions, and try a writing activity.

AV² Quiz
Take this quiz to test your knowledge

Due to the dynamic nature of the Internet, some of the URLs and activities provided as part of AV² by Weigl may have changed or ceased to exist. AV² by Weigl accepts no responsibility for any such changes. All media enhanced books ar regularly monitored to update addresses and sites in a timely manner. Contact AV² by Weigl at 1-866-649-3445 or av2books@weigl.com with any questions, comments, or feedback.